Color Me, Fold Me
Coloring Book

Christmas Edition
Volume 1

by Ruby Phoenix

Color Me, Fold Me Coloring Book, Volume 1
Copyright © 2016 by Ruby Phoenix
Cover designed by Leuchi through DesignCrowd

Facebook: www.facebook.com/rubyphoenix8/

Instagram: www.instagram.com/phoenixruby/

Twitter: www.twitter.com/phoenixruby11/

SPECIAL NOTE

The pages of this book are suitable for alcohol free markers,
colored pencils and more due to single sided pages.

If using markers, the color may bleed through so place a blank
sheet of paper (preferably heavy duty) or cardboard between
the pages when coloring.

Color me – Fold me Concept

CURRENTLY:

☺ Before CHRISTMAS

☺ CHRISTMAS

☹ After CHRISTMAS

COLOR ME – FOLD ME EFFECT:

☺ Before CHRISTMAS	Color shapes in the COLOR ME, FOLD ME coloring book, make decorations and fill them with small Christmas gifts
☺ CHRISTMAS	Enjoy Christmas with your own uniquely decorated Christmas tree right at the centre of your home – be proud
☺ After CHRISTMAS	Take down the Christmas tree, and ask family members and friends to unwrap decorations to reveal the gifts

Color and craft your own decorations, hide small gifts in them and make the January Christmas tree taking down a special family occasion – "Blue Monday" doesn't need to be depressing.

STEP 1:
Color recyclable Christmas tree decoration templates throughout the autumn months.

STEP 2:
Before Christmas, cut the colored templates out and make your own decorations.

> **STEP 2a:**
> Hide candies, coins, banknotes, engagement ring and other small surprise gifts within the
decorations.

STEP 3:
Enjoy Christmas and your fabulously decorated Christmas tree, hiding little treasures in the decorations.

Step 4:
January is the most depressing month of the year and taking down Christmas tree – knowing the fun is over – contributes to that. Ask family members to take down the Christmas tree, unwrapping decorations to find the hidden "Happy New Year" surprise gifts (candies, coins, banknotes, engagement ring, etc.).

Tools & Materials

Coloring
Best results are achieved with alcohol free marker pens or coloring pencils.

Suggestions for colored pencils:
        Beginners: Sargent Art 50-count and Staedtler Ergosoft;
        Advanced: Prismacolor Premier Soft Core (132 colored pencils)
Suggestions for markers:
        Staedtler Triplus Fineliner Markers
        Sakura Gelly Roll Gel Pens

Cutting
Scissors and retractable utility knife. I use IKEA dressmaking scissors (high quality scissors recommendation: Fiskars Dressmaking Scissors).

Scissors: CAUTION Cut Hazard: Scissors have functional sharp edges. Contact may result in injury. Always keep blades away from fingers and body. Handle with care. Use with adult supervision. Not for ages 12 and under.

Retractable utility knife: CAUTION Cut Hazard: Sharp blades. Improper use, chiseling, ice picking, prying, applying force onto back of blade (or anywhere else for that matter), or contact may result in injury. Always keep blades away from fingers and body. Do not use if damaged or blade is loose. Handle with care. If not in use, retract the blade and store in a safe place. **Keep out of reach of children.**

Gluing
Paper glue: I recommend Saunders UHU Glue stick (99655) for larger applications and Aleenes 15599 All Purpose Glue (Original Tacky Glue) for higher precision applications either directly from the bottle or brushed onto the surface.

Use Scotch Quick Dry Tacky Glue/Adhesive (4 ounces; 59ml) to glue together 5-point and 6-point star halves or for any other application where quick drying is required.

Decorating tree
Buy decorative strings (local art shop) or you can make your own paper strings using the leftover paper from cutting shapes.

Test Page

Just in case – test your colored pencils and markers on this page before coloring Christmas tree decorations.

SPECIAL NOTE: To prevent bleed-through when coloring, place a blank sheet of heavy duty paper or cardboard between the pages when coloring.

BLEEDING-THROUGH TEST PAGE

Color in shapes on the test page using a variety of markers and check this page for any bleeding through the paper.

Christmas Tree Decorations

The following pages contain instructions and shapes for Christmas tree decorations. Color in the shapes first, cut them out and finally fold and glue to create your own Christmas tree decorations.

Instructions

INSTRUCTIONS ❶
South American panpipes

Roll out the cut-out with a round pen to achieve rolled shape (see image below). Use the flaps ("handles") for easier rolling and gluing.

Once each pipe is created, cut the extending flaps with scissors.

Arrange pipes to face images as desired and apply glue first to the side of the small pipe before applying it to the next larger pipe and so on. Glue needs to dry before continuing with other pipes.

Create holes on the shortest and longest pipe (see below). Run through the hanging string.

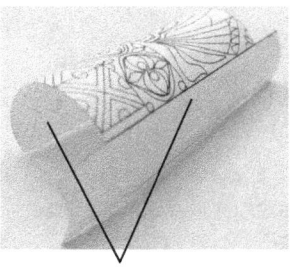

APPLY GLUE HERE

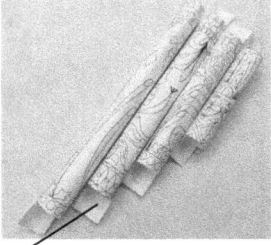

CUT AWAY EXTENDING FLAPS

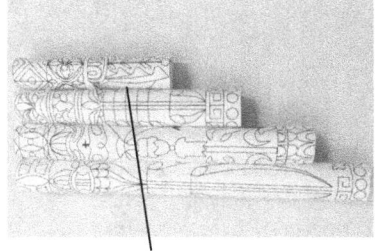

Run the string through the holes on both sides

APPLY GLUE TO THE SIDE & PRESS TWO TUBES TOGETHER (wait for the glue to dry)
You may wish to place a gift (e.g. rolled up bank note) into one of the tubes.

INSTRUCTIONS ❷
Box

Cut the shape from the coloring book page and fold as shown in the image below. The top cover (the one with no gluing flaps) should be glued last.

When the sides of the box are glued, place a gift and the hanging string into the box as shown below and glue the top side to the flaps.

Hang the box decoration with a hidden gift above a fireplace or on your Christmas tree to be ready for the January surprise taking down.

APPLY GLUE HERE (OUTSIDE) TO THE SIDE FLAPS FIRST (THE TOP SIDE IS GLUED LAST)

APPLY GLUE HERE AND CLOSE THE TOP SO IT IS GLUED TO THE THREE FLAPS.

BOX CAN HANG IN DIFFERENT WAYS (e.g. CORNER & MIDDLE OF THE SIDE)

INSTRUCTIONS ❸

Single cone and two-sided cone

Cut the shape from the coloring book page and roll as shown in the image below (cut the tip of the cone – needed to run through the hanging string.

Push the string through the tip of the cone and fold each petal/flap to form a shape as shown in the image below (don't forget to insert a small gift prior to gluing the cones together).

Hang the decoration with a hidden gift on your Christmas tree (or above the fireplace).

Single cone I.: apply glue to 4 petals on the round base and attach to the cone (inside).

Single cone II.: apply glue to petals on the round base and the cone (with a gift inside).

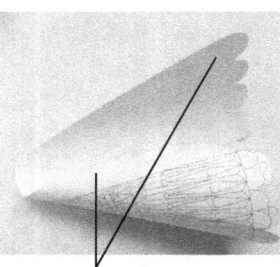

APPLY GLUE HERE AND BRING THE SIDES TOGETHER TO FORM A CONE.

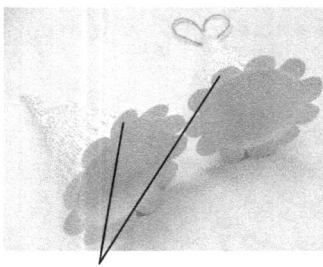

APPLY GLUE TO PETALS AND GLUE TWO CONES TOGETHER.

FINAL RESULT.

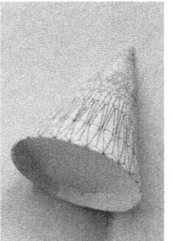

PLACE A GIFT INS THE CONE BEFORE GLUING.

GLUE THE BASE AND THE CONE (see above).

INSTRUCTIONS ❹

Eight- and twelve-petal bulb

Cut the shape from the coloring book page and fold as shown in the image below. Run each petal between your thumb and a ruler to curl them as shown below.

Overlap the petals as shown below and secure with the hanging string (upside position). Don't forget to place a small gift in the bulb before securing!

The decorative bulb can also be hanged upside down. See the previous image on how to close and secure the bulb (again, don't forget the gift!).

BULBS CAN STAND UPSIDE LIKE THIS – THERE IS ENOUGH SPACE FOR A SMALL GIFT.

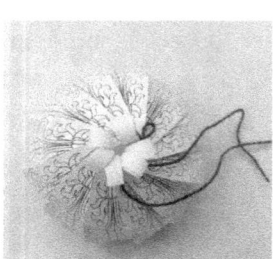

FOLD ONE PETAL AFTER ANOTHER (TIPS HAVE TO BE CURLED OUTWARDS).

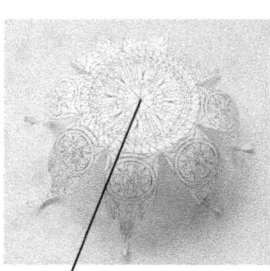

CREATE A SMALL HOLE IN THE MIDDLE AND RUN THROUGH THE HANGING STRING.

INSTRUCTIONS ❺
Cylinder

Cut the shape from the coloring book page and roll as shown in the image below (rolling makes it easier to close the cylinder).

Cut top and bottom covers and glue the bottom cover to the main body of the cylinder (place a small gift inside once the bottom cover is glued onto the cylinder).

Hang the cylinder decoration with a hidden gift above a fireplace or on your Christmas tree to be ready for the January surprise taking down.

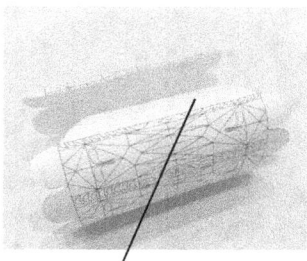

APPLY GLUE HERE AND BRING TWO SIDES TOGETHER TO FORM A CYLINDER

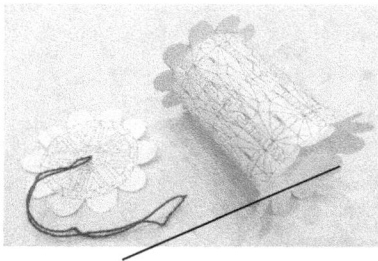

APPLY GLUE TO EXTENSION PETALS AND ATTACH THE TOP COVER (THE ONE WITH THE DECORATIVE HANGING STRING).

FINAL RESULT: CYLINDER IN ITS VERTICAL POSITION.

INSTRUCTIONS ❻
Drum

Cut the shape (main body, covers and decorative paper ribbon) from the coloring book page and roll as shown in the image below.

Apply glue to flaps (see below) and attach to the body one by one around the perimeter.

Covers have to be attached first. Close the body by gluing flaps to the inside of the body (see the first image).

Use the decorative paper ribbon, apply some glue to it and wrap it around the centre of the main body of the drum (see image below).

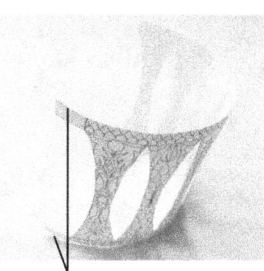

GLUE TO BE APPLIED ON THESE FLAPS WHEN THE COVERS ARE ATTACHED TO THE BODY

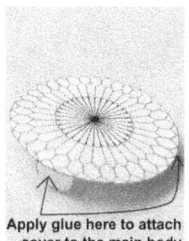

Apply glue here to attach cover to the main body

APPLY GLUE TO FLAPS ONE BY ONE ON BOTH COVERS

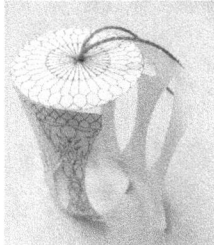

ATTACH BOTH COVERS TO THE BODY BEFORE CLOSING IT

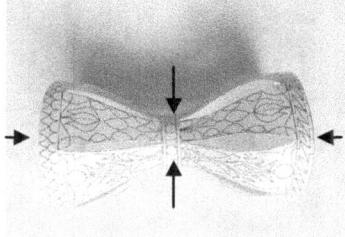

APPLY GLUE TO ONE END OF THE RIBBON AND SQUEEZE THE MAIN BODY OF THE DRUM BEFORE WRAPPING AND SECURING.

Large & small stars (5-point & 6-point)

Cut the 5 or 6 shapes (points of a star) from the coloring book page and fold as shown below. Two flaps on a 6-point star have to completely overlap when gluing (5-point star: see image below).

Apply glue to the outside of the centre flaps as shown below and glue them together (one by one). These centre flaps will make the star shape sturdier.

When the halves of the star are finished (see below), place in the hanging string, apply liquid and fast drying glue to the star point flaps, and bring them together to form a 3-D star.

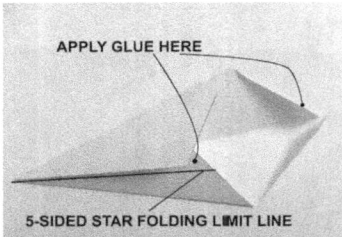

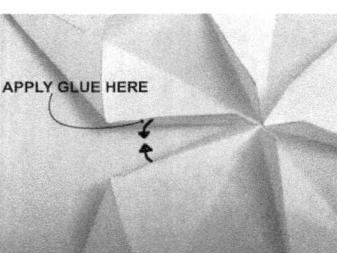

APPLY GLUE ON THE INNER FLAP TO THE FOLDING LIMIT LINE (5-POINT STAR) OR ACROSS THE WHOLE INNER FLAP (6-POINT STAR)

APPLY GLUE AS SHOWN AND HOLD FLAPS TOGETHER TO FORM A STRONG BOND

APPLY GLUE HERE (ON EACH POINT) AND HOLD TWO HALVES TOGETHER TO FORM A STRONG BOND

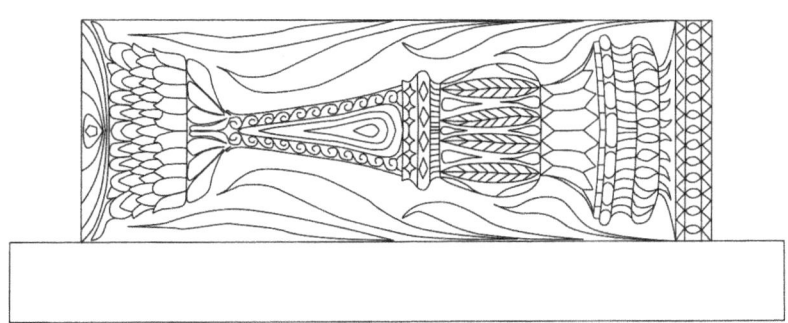

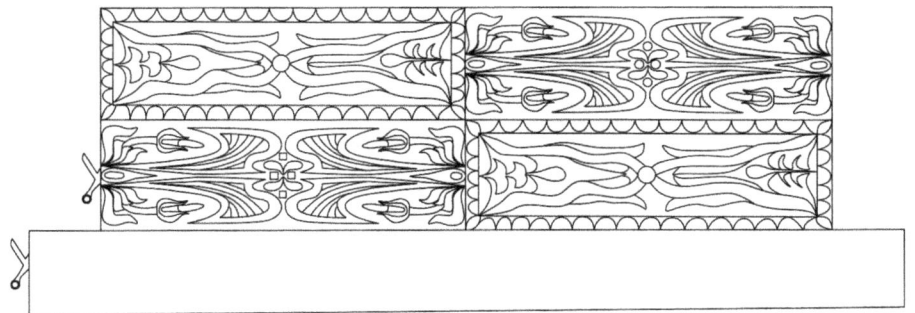

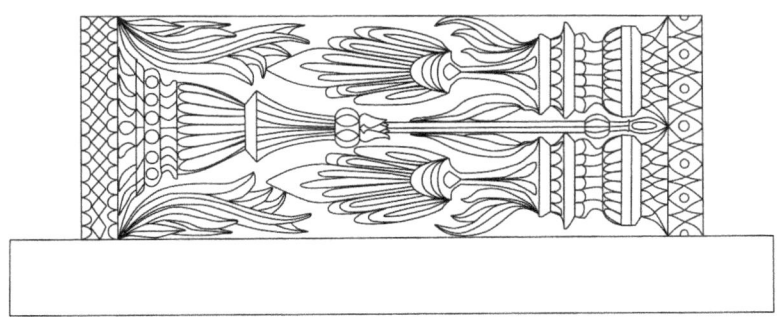

✂ - Cut the shapes out after coloring as indicated above
Recommended glue: Saunders UHU Glue stick (99655)

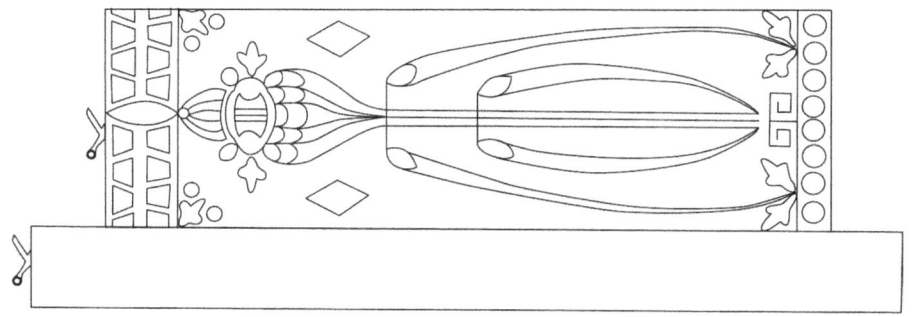

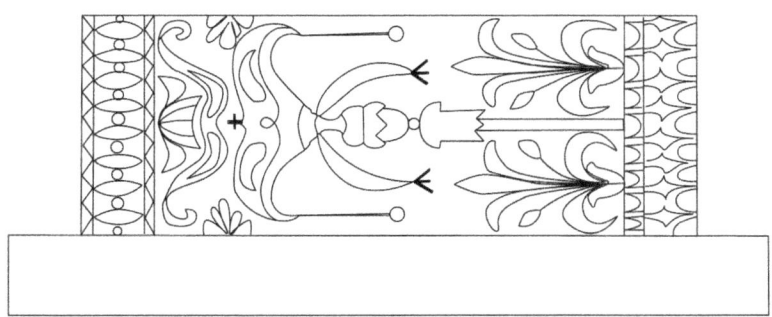

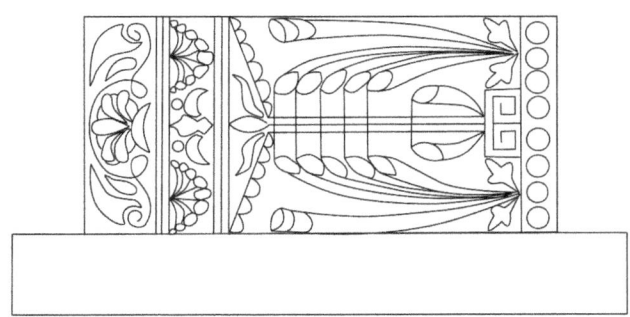

INSTRUCTIONS ❷

✂ - Cut the shapes out after coloring as indicated above
Recommended glue: Aleenes 15599 All Purpose Glue

✄ - Cut the shapes out after coloring as indicated above
Recommended glue: Aleenes 15599 All Purpose Glue

✂ - Cut the shapes out after coloring as indicated above
Recommended glue: Aleenes 15599 All Purpose Glue

INSTRUCTIONS ❸

✂ - Cut the shapes out after coloring as indicated above
Recommended glue: Saunders UHU Glue stick (99655)

INSTRUCTIONS ❸

✂ - Cut the shapes out after coloring as indicated above
Recommended glue: Saunders UHU Glue stick (99655)

✂ - Cut the shapes out after coloring as indicated above
Recommended glue: Saunders UHU Glue stick (99655)

✂ - Cut the shapes out after coloring as indicated above
Recommended glue: Saunders UHU Glue stick (99655)

 - Cut the shapes out after coloring as indicated above
Recommended glue: Saunders UHU Glue stick (99655)

✂ - Cut the shapes out after coloring as indicated above
Recommended glue: Saunders UHU Glue stick (99655)

INSTRUCTIONS ❹

✄ - Cut the shapes out after coloring as indicated above

INSTRUCTIONS ❹

✂ - Cut the shapes out after coloring as indicated above

INSTRUCTIONS ❹

✂ - Cut the shapes out after coloring as indicated above

✂ - Cut the shapes out after coloring as indicated above

✂ - Cut the shapes out after coloring as indicated above

✂ - Cut the shapes out after coloring as indicated above
Recommended glue: Saunders UHU Glue stick (99655)

✂ - Cut the shapes out after coloring as indicated above
Recommended glue: Saunders UHU Glue stick (99655)

✂ - Cut the shapes out after coloring as indicated above
Recommended glue: Saunders UHU Glue stick (99655)

✂ - Cut the shapes out after coloring as indicated above
Recommended glue: Saunders UHU Glue stick (99655)

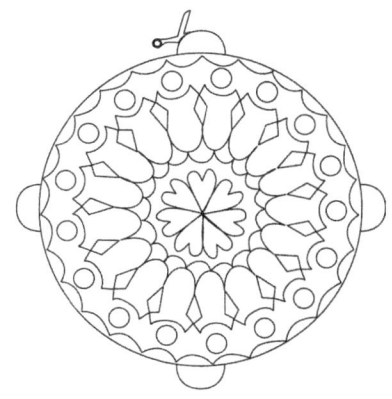

✂ - Cut the shapes out after coloring as indicated above
Recommended glue: Saunders UHU Glue stick (99655)

INSTRUCTIONS ❻

✂ - Cut the shapes out after coloring as indicated above
Recommended glue: Saunders UHU Glue stick (99655)

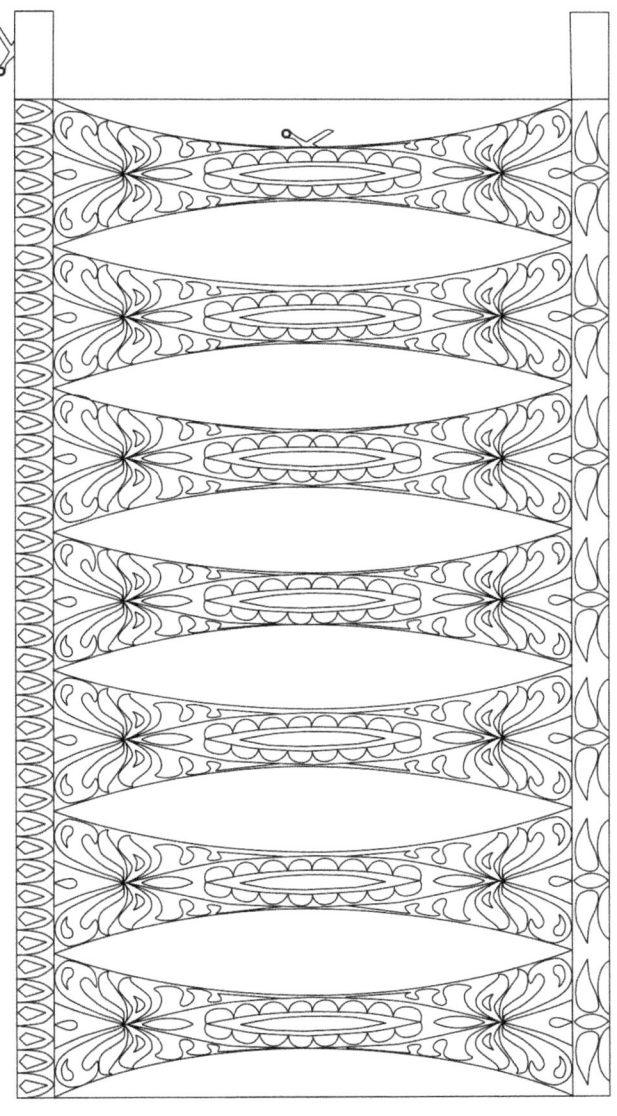

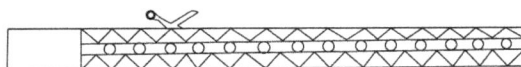

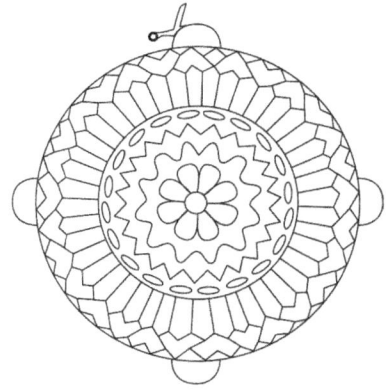

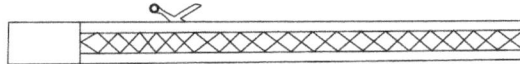

✂ - Cut the shapes out after coloring as indicated above
Recommended glue: Saunders UHU Glue stick (99655)

INSTRUCTIONS ➐

✂ - Cut the shapes out
after coloring as
indicated above
Recommended glue:
Saunders UHU Glue
stick (99655)
Scotch Quick Dry Tacky
Glue/Adhesive

INSTRUCTIONS ❼

✂ - Cut the shapes out after coloring as indicated above
Recommended glue:
Saunders UHU Glue stick (99655)
Scotch Quick Dry Tacky Glue/Adhesive

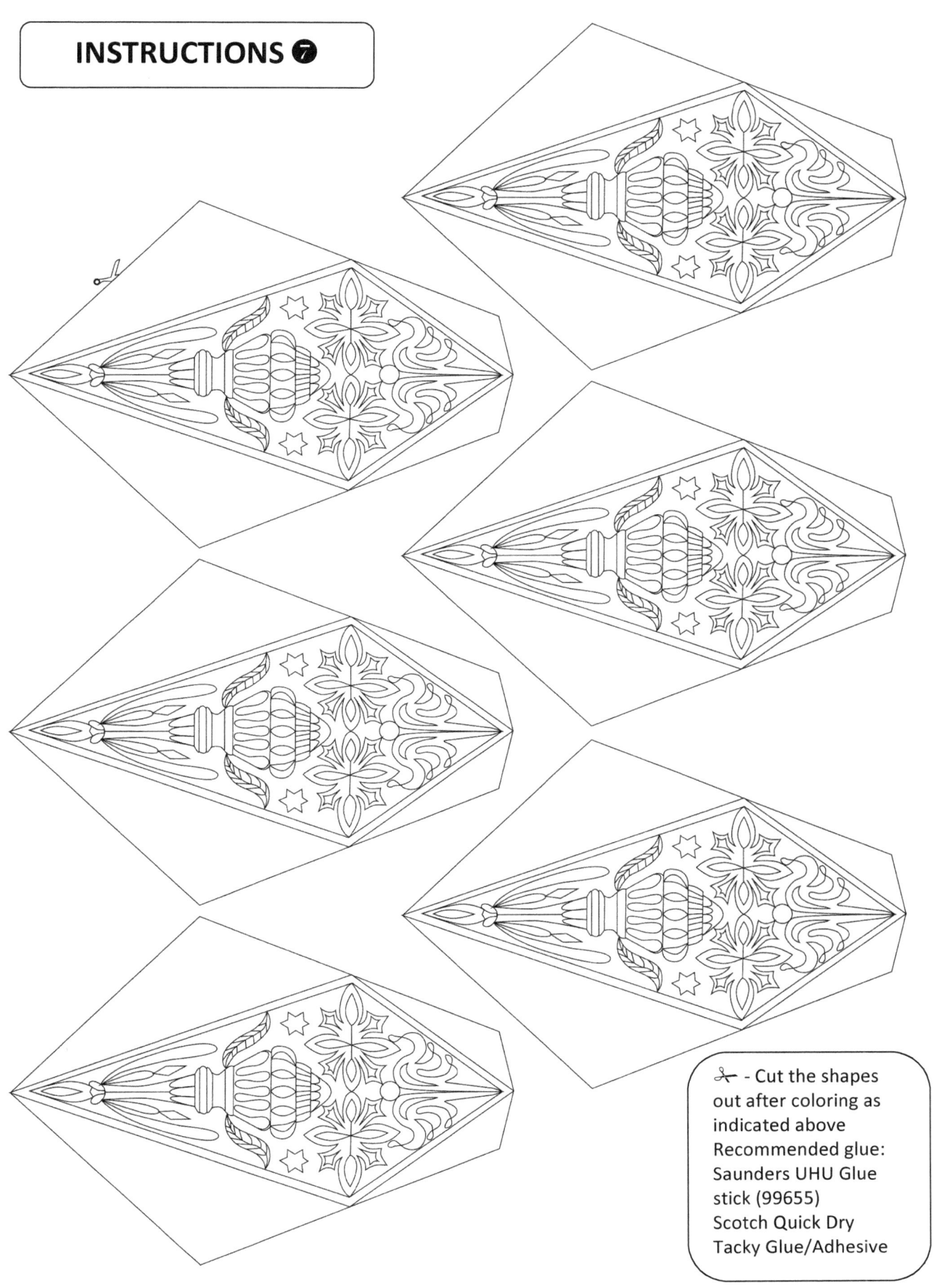

INSTRUCTIONS ➐

✂ - Cut the shapes out after coloring as indicated above
Recommended glue:
Saunders UHU Glue stick (99655)
Scotch Quick Dry Tacky Glue/Adhesive

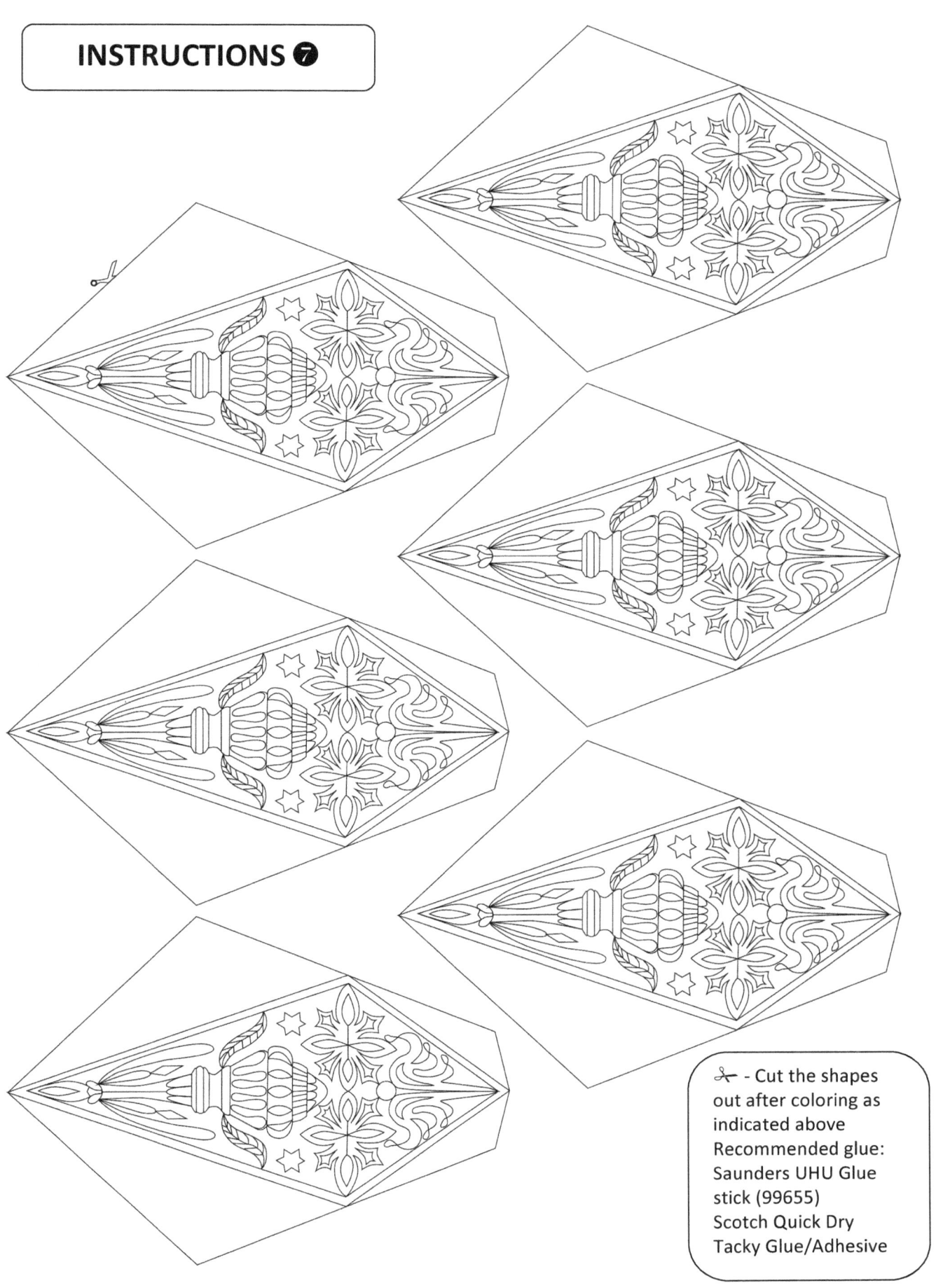

INSTRUCTIONS ❼

✂ - Cut the shapes
out after coloring as
indicated above
Recommended glue:
Saunders UHU Glue
stick (99655)
Scotch Quick Dry
Tacky Glue/Adhesive

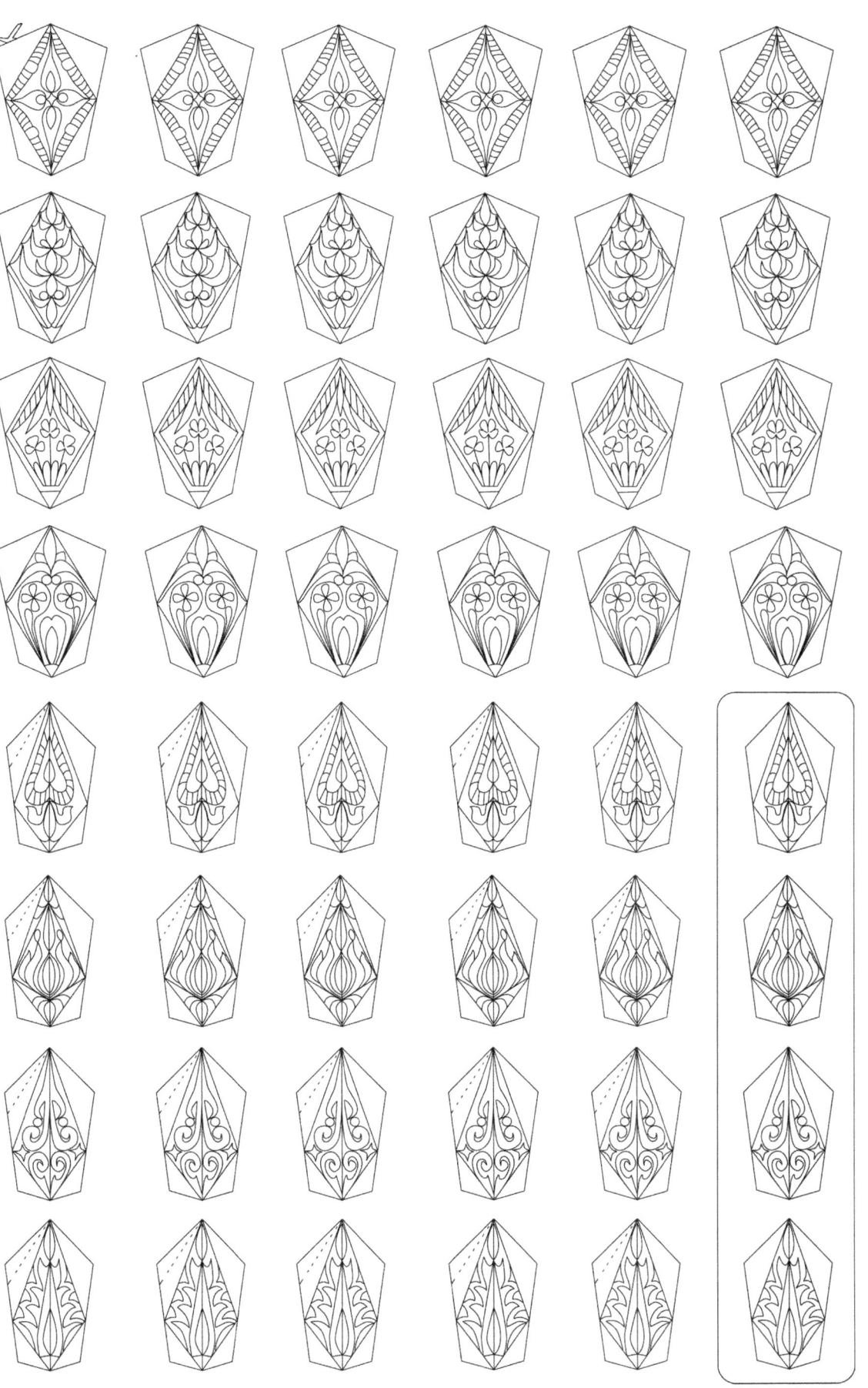

✂ – Cut the shapes out after coloring as indicated above
Recommended glue: Saunders UHU Glue stick (99655)
Scotch Quick Dry Tacky Glue/Adhesive

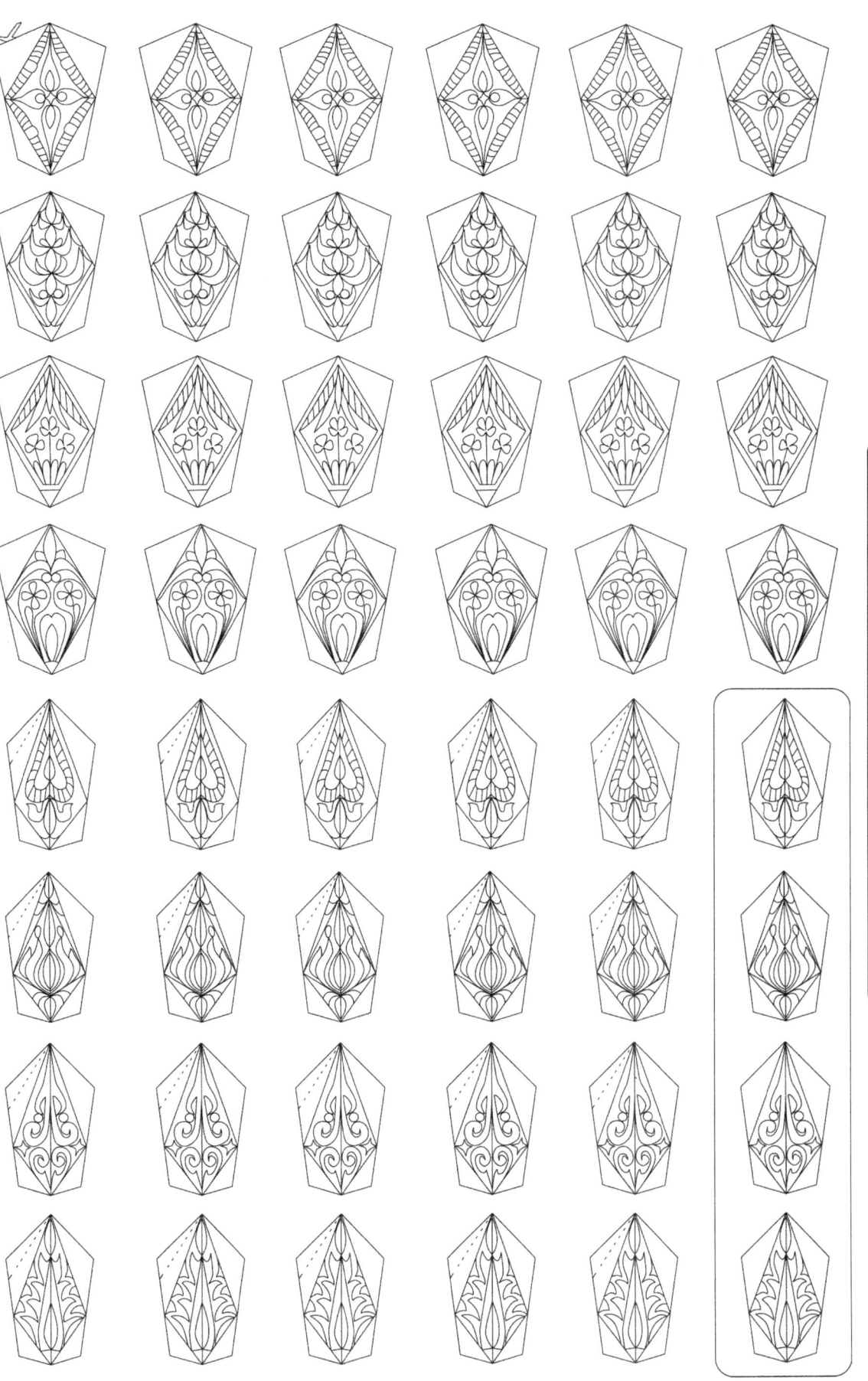

INSTRUCTIONS ➐

✄ - Cut the shapes out after coloring as indicated above
Recommended glue: Saunders UHU Glue stick (99655)
Scotch Quick Dry Tacky Glue/Adhesive

After Christmas Coloring

The following pages are for coloring enthusiasts, containing shapes from the cone decorations and do not require any cutting and gluing – unless you wish to frame the colored in shapes.

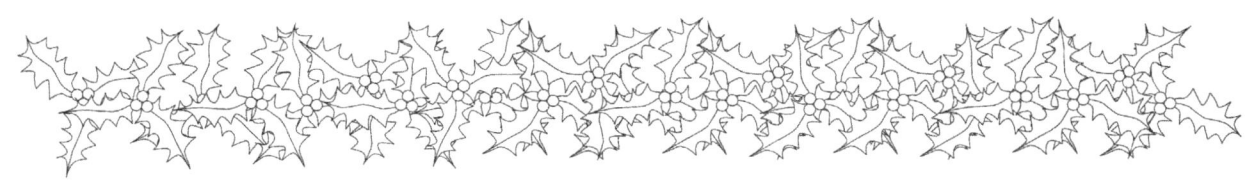